D1736544

Take Care of
THE EARTH
Every Day

by Tammy Gagne

amicus
high interest

Amicus High Interest is published by Amicus
P.O. Box 1329, Mankato, MN 56002
www.amicuspublishing.us

Library of Congress Cataloging-in-Publication Data
Gagne, Tammy.
  Take care of the earth every day / Tammy Gagne.
      pages cm. -- (Kids save the earth)
  ISBN 978-1-60753-521-8 (hardcover : alk paper) -- ISBN 978-1-60753-551-5
(eBook)
  1. Environmentalism--Juvenile literature. I. Title.
  GE195.5.G36 2014
  363.7--dc23
                                    2013008496

Photo Credits: Alex Staroseltsev/Shutterstock Images, cover; Shutterstock
Images, 2, 13, 20; Mikael Damkier/Shutterstock Images, 5; Gyuszko Photo/
Shutterstock Images, 6; Joe Belanger/Shutterstock Images, 9; RT Images/
Shutterstock Images, 10; Sari Oneal/Shutterstock Images, 14; Hung
Chung Chih/Shutterstock Images, 17; Red Line Editorial, 19

Produced for Amicus by The Peterson Publishing Company
and Red Line Editorial.

Editor Jenna Gleisner
Designer Becky Daum
Printed in the United States of America
Mankato, MN
12-2013
PO1187
10 9 8 7 6 5 4 3 2

TABLE OF CONTENTS

Earth Is Our Home   4

Air Pollution   6

Recycle   8

Keep Earth Clean   10

Don't Waste Food   12

Care for Animals and Plants   14

Work Together   16

Plant a Tree   18

Earth Day   20

Get Started Today   22

Words to Know   23

Learn More   24

Index   24

EARTH IS OUR HOME

The earth belongs to us all. It is where we live, play, and learn. It is our home. We need to take good care of the earth.

AIR POLLUTION

Some things **pollute** the earth. Most cars run on gas. Using gas pollutes the air. **Hybrid cars** can run on electricity and gas. This is better for the earth.

Let's Do It

Walk or ride your bike. This is not bad for the air at all!

RECYCLE

You can **recycle** to help care for the earth. This uses old items to make new ones. Bottles and jars can be made into new things. It makes less trash. Less trash means less pollution.

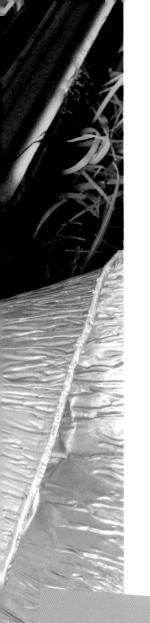

KEEP EARTH CLEAN

Trash can pollute our water. Then it is not safe to drink. We can help. Clean up litter. This will help keep our water clean.

Let's Do It

Always put your trash in a bin. Pick up trash you see.

DON'T WASTE FOOD

Food comes from the earth. We must not waste it. Wasted food becomes trash. Always eat what is on your plate. Only take what you need.

CARE FOR ANIMALS AND PLANTS

Animals and plants live here, too. Care for all living things. It is part of taking care of the earth.

Let's Do It

Many animals make their homes in trees. But trees are often cut down. Make a birdhouse. This gives birds a safe place to live.

WORK TOGETHER

Some animals are **endangered**. They may need our help. Join a club that helps animals. Help save their **habitat**, or home.

PLANT A TREE

Plant a tree to help the earth. Plants and trees can be a home for many animals. They also help keep the air clean.

How It Works

Plants use up a gas called carbon dioxide. Then they put oxygen back in the air. We need this to breathe. So do animals.

How a Plant Makes Oxygen

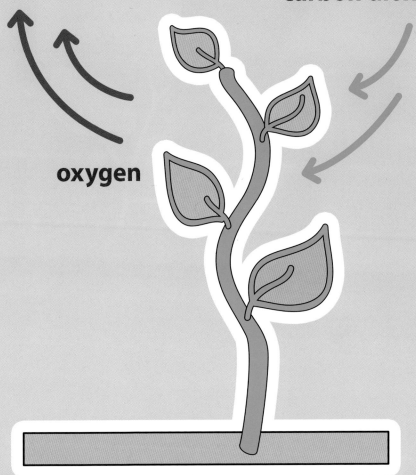

carbon dioxide

oxygen

EARTH DAY

Earth Day is April 22 every year. Join in. Get a group together. Pick up litter. Plant trees. Have fun taking care of the earth together.

There is only one Earth. We can all help keep it clean. How do you take care of the earth?

GET STARTED TODAY

- Walk or ride your bike.

- Recycle items you use.

- Do not litter.

- Pick up when others litter.

- Make a birdhouse.

- Plant a tree.

WORDS TO KNOW

carbon dioxide – a gas that humans and animals breathe out while plants take it in

endangered – in danger of becoming extinct

habitat – the place where an animal or plant makes its home

hybrid car – a car that can get its power from electricity and gas

oxygen – a gas that humans and animals need to breathe

pollute – to make something dirty

recycle – to process old items, such as glass, plastic, cans, and paper, so they can be used to make new items

LEARN MORE

Books

Frantz, Jennifer. *Earth Day Fun*. New York: HarperCollins, 2011.

Hewitt, Sally. *Caring for Our Earth*. Mankato, MN: Amicus, 2011.

Web Sites

EcoKids
http://www.ecokids.ca/pub/index.cfm
Play games, read stories, and learn facts about saving the earth.

PBS Kids
http://pbskids.org/games/earthday.html
Play fun Earth Day games, and learn new ways to take care of the earth.

Planetpals
http://www.planetpals.com/
Learn more about Earth Day, recycling, and endangered species.

INDEX

air, 7, 18
animals, 15, 16, 18

carbon dioxide, 18, 19

Earth Day, 21

gas, 7, 18

hybrid cars, 7

litter, 11, 21

oxygen, 18, 19

plants, 15, 18
pollution, 7, 8, 11

recycling, 8

trash, 8, 11, 12
trees, 15, 18, 21